WAR MACHINES ARMORED PERSONNEL CARRIERS

The M113

by Michael and Gladys Green

Capstone
press
Mankato, Minnesota

Edge Books are published by Capstone Press,
151 Good Counsel Drive, P.O. Box 669, Mankato, Minnesota 56002.
www.capstonepress.com

Library of Congress Cataloging-in-Publication Data
Green, Michael, 1952–
    Armored personnel carriers: the M113 / by Michael and Gladys Green.
    p. cm.—(Edge books. War machines)
    Includes bibliographical references and index.
    ISBN 0-7368-3777-9 (hardcover)
    1. M113 (Armored personnel carrier)—Juvenile literature. I. Green, Gladys,
1954– II. Title. III. Edge Books, war machines.
UG446.5.G73297 2005
623.7'475—dc22   2004012156

Summary: Describes the M113 Armored Personnel Carrier, including its history,
equipment, weapons, tactics, and future use.

Editorial Credits
Angie Kaelberer, editor; Jason Knudson, set designer; Patrick D. Dentinger, book designer;
    Ted Williams, illustrator; Jo Miller, photo researcher; Scott Thoms, photo editor

Photo Credits
Corbis, 6, 17; Bettmann, 7; Leif Skoogfors, 14
DVIC, 11, 12; Ben Andrade, 22; Joint Service Audiovisual Team, cover; Master SGT
    Herbert Cintron, 21; SSGT Russ Pollanen, 24
Getty Images Inc./Justin Sullivan, 5; U.S. Army/Joseph Robert, 27
Michael Green, 18–19
United Defense, L.P., 9, 13
Zuma Press/San Antonio Express/B. M. Sobhani, 28

Capstone Press thanks Scott Gourley for his assistance with this book.

1 2 3 4 5 6 10 09 08 07 06 05

Table of Contents

CHAPTER 1

The M113 in Action

Three enemy soldiers hide near a road. They plan to fire on a group of U.S. Army trucks carrying supplies to a nearby base. The trucks have no armor to protect them.

As the Army trucks come closer, the enemy soldiers open fire with machine guns and rifles. The truck drivers try to turn their vehicles around. But they are trapped. Just then, a U.S. Army M113 Armored Personnel Carrier (APC) rushes to the rescue.

A soldier on the M113 fires a machine gun at the enemy soldiers. The enemy soldiers return fire. Their bullets bounce off the armored hull of the M113. A large ramp at the rear of the M113 drops down, and 11 soldiers rush out. They surround the enemy soldiers.

The enemy soldiers throw down their weapons. The supply trucks continue their drive to the base.

An M113's armor protects it from bullets.

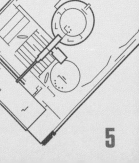

LEARN ABOUT:

A daring rescue

Off-road vehicles

The first M113s

In World War II, the Army needed a faster vehicle to keep up with tanks.

The Need

The U.S. Army first used tanks during World War I (1914–1918). Soldiers could walk as fast as the slow-moving tanks. When the Army built faster tanks, it needed a vehicle to move soldiers at the same speed. Tanks built just to carry soldiers cost too much money. Trucks could carry soldiers. But most trucks couldn't go off-road.

In the late 1930s, the Army began using a different type of truck. Tracks replaced the truck's rear wheels. The Army called this vehicle a half-track.

Half-tracks carried soldiers during World War II.

During World War II (1939–1945), the Army used thousands of half-tracks to carry soldiers. The half-tracks were still much slower than tanks on rough ground. The Army then developed an armored personnel carrier. This vehicle had full tracks. The Army began using the APCs in the 1950s.

The M113 is the most successful Army APC. The Army started using it in 1960. The newest version of the vehicle is called the M113A3. A company called United Defense builds the M113 APCs.

The M113A3 is the newest
M113 model.

CHAPTER 2

Inside the M113

The M113 APC acts like a battlefield taxi. It brings soldiers into battle behind tanks. The soldiers leave the APC and fight on foot.

The M113 APC is able to travel through almost any area. It runs smoothly over sand or mud. It even floats in deep water.

Engine

The M113's engine is in the front of the vehicle. Early M113s had a 209-horsepower gasoline engine. This engine gave the M113 a top speed of about 37 miles (60 kilometers) per hour.

Range is the distance a vehicle can travel on one tank of fuel. The first M113s had a range of about 200 miles (322 kilometers).

The M113 floats in water.

LEARN ABOUT:

A battlefield taxi

Parts

Crew members

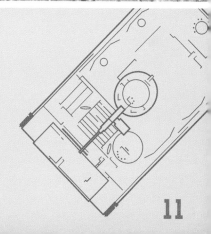

Diesel Engine

In 1964, the Army started using a new model of the M113 APC. The new M113A1 had a diesel engine instead of a gasoline engine. It produced 212 horsepower.

The diesel engine had several advantages. Diesel engines run longer on less fuel than gasoline engines. The M113A1's range is about 300 miles (480 kilometers). It has a top speed of 37 miles (60 kilometers) per hour.

Diesel engines made the M113A1 safer for the crew.

The diesel engine also lowered the fire danger to the crew and passengers. Diesel is less likely to catch fire than gasoline.

The M113A3 has a turbo supercharged diesel engine. This engine takes in more air and fuel than a regular diesel engine. As a result, it produces 275 horsepower. Its top speed is 41 miles (66 kilometers) per hour. Its range is the same as that of the M113A1.

In safe areas, the crew opens the
roof hatches to see out of the vehicle.

Suspension System

M113s ride into action on road wheels. These wheels are covered with rubber. Two sets of flexible steel and rubber tracks enclose the road wheels. The tracks spread the vehicle's weight over the ground, much like a snowshoe does for a person.

Each of the road wheels connects to a steel bar called a torsion bar. The torsion bars absorb bumps to make the ride smoother for the crew.

Driver Position

The driver sits in the front hull next to the engine. An opening called a roof hatch is above the driver's seat.

In combat areas, the crew keeps the hatch closed. The driver steers by looking through periscopes. In safe areas, the driver can open the roof hatch. At night, the driver uses night vision devices to see.

Other Crew Positions

The M113 APC commander sits in the center of the vehicle. A second roof hatch is over the commander's seat. The roof hatch is open unless the M113 is under heavy enemy fire. The commander stands on the seat to look out.

The commander and driver wear helmets. These helmets have a built-in intercom system. The commander and driver use the intercom system to talk to each other.

The rear hull holds 11 soldiers. The back of the hull opens to form a ramp. Soldiers use the ramp to enter and leave the M113.

The back of the rear hull opens to form a ramp.

MII3A3

Function:	Armored Personnel Carrier
Manufacturer:	United Defense Ground Systems Division
Entered Service:	1987
Length:	16 feet (4.9 meters)
Width:	8.8 feet (2.7 meters)
Height:	7.2 feet (2.2 meters)
Weight:	27,180 pounds (12,329 kilograms)
Engine:	Detroit Diesel 6V53T
Horsepower:	275
Speed:	41 miles (66 kilometers) per hour
Range:	300 miles (480 kilometers)

2

1

1 Smoke grenade launchers

2 Machine gun

3 Roof hatch

4 Road wheels

5 Tracks

6 Radio antenna

7 Hull

CHAPTER 3

Weapons and Tactics

The M113 APC's main weapon is the M2 .50-caliber machine gun. The M2 is mounted on top of the hull.

The M2 weighs 84 pounds (38 kilograms). It is too heavy for one person to carry and fire. Instead, vehicles like the M113 carry it. The gun fires 450 to 550 rounds per minute. It can hit targets as far away as 6,500 feet (2,000 meters).

During the Vietnam War (1954–1975), the Army added two 7.62 mm machine guns to the M113's rear hull. These M60 machine guns fire 450 to 600 rounds per minute. Their range is about 3,600 feet (1,100 meters).

The M2 machine gun is mounted on the M113's hull.

LEARN ABOUT:

Machine guns

Missiles and mortars

Battle leaders

Missile Carrier

In the early 1970s, the Army added an antitank missile to the M113 APC. This missile was the Tube-launched, Optically-tracked, Wire command-link missile system (TOW).

The TOW launcher sat in the rear hull of the M113. Crew members had to open the M113's roof hatch to fire the missiles.

In the early 1980s, the Army improved the design. It called the new vehicle the M901/M901A1 Improved TOW Vehicle (ITV). This vehicle is safer for the crew. Crew members stay inside the vehicle's hull. They fire the missiles by remote control.

The newest version is the M901A3 ITV. This model has the improvements found in the M113A3.

The Army added antitank missiles to the M113 (left) and improved the design with the M901 (right).

Mortars

In the early 1960s, the Army added small cannons called mortars to two M113 models. The models were the M125 and the M106.

In the 1980s, the Army stopped using the M125s. It replaced the 107 mm mortar on the M106 with a 120 mm mortar. The 120 mm

mortar is larger and more powerful than the 107 mm mortar. The Army called the new vehicle the M1064A3 mortar carrier. Its mortar hits targets nearly 5 miles (8 kilometers) away.

The M1064A3 has four crew members. The crew includes a squad leader, a gunner, and an assistant gunner. The fourth crew member serves as ammunition bearer, operator, and driver.

Tactics

Designers wanted to keep the M113's weight as low as possible. The vehicle has very thin aluminum armor. The armor protects the vehicle from small bullets. Crews use trees, hills, and other natural features to hide from larger bullets and bombs.

M113s often travel to battle sites with tanks. In unsafe areas, the M113s drive in front of the tanks. Soldiers aboard the M113s search the area for hidden enemy soldiers.

The M106 had a 107 mm cannon.

CHAPTER 4

The Future

Since 1960, United Defense has built about 80,000 M113 APCs. At least 50 armies around the world use the vehicle.

Changes

The U.S. Army and United Defense continue to improve the M113. The newest version is called the M113A3 APC.

The A3 has new safety features. On earlier models, enemy weapons could hit the fuel stored inside and cause the vehicle to explode. On the A3, the two fuel tanks are on the outside of the rear hull. If the fuel tanks explode, the soldiers will be safe.

The M113A3's fuel tanks are outside of the hull.

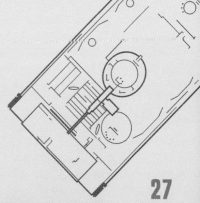

LEARN ABOUT:

A worldwide vehicle

Improvements

Computer and GPS systems

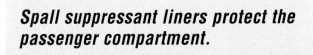

Spall suppressant liners protect the passenger compartment.

Spall suppressant liners inside the rear hull protect soldiers from small bits of ammunition called spall. The liners are thin, flat panels made of bulletproof material. The liners are mounted on tracks. The crew can open and close them as needed.

New Computer

Some of the M113A3s have a computer. The computer uses a Global Positioning System (GPS) to locate military vehicles and soldiers. Its monitor has a map that is constantly updated. This map shows the position of friendly and enemy units. The computer also sends and receives pictures and messages through a wireless Internet system.

The U.S. Army had about 33,000 M113 APCs in service in the early 1980s. By 2003, that number had dropped to about 14,000. The Army now uses newer vehicles to perform many jobs once done by the M113s. But the M113s are so dependable that the Army plans to keep them in service for many more years.

Glossary

aluminum (uh-LOO-mi-nuhm)—a strong, lightweight metal

ammunition (am-yuh-NISH-uhn)—bullets and other objects that are fired from weapons

armor (AR-mur)—a protective metal covering

caliber (KAH-luh-bur)—the diameter of the inside of a gun's barrel

diesel (DEE-zuhl)—a heavy fuel that burns to make power

horsepower (HORSS-pou-ur)—a unit for measuring an engine's power

periscope (PER-uh-skope)—a viewing device with mirrors at each end

spall (SPAHL)—small bits of ammunition

torsion bar (TOR-shuhn BAHR)—a long, narrow piece of metal that has one end attached to the frame of an M113 and the other to the wheel axle

Read More

Graham, Ian. *Military Vehicles.* Designed for Success. Chicago: Heinemann, 2003.

Green, Michael, and Greg Stewart. *Modern U.S. Tanks and AFVs.* Enthusiast Color. St. Paul, Minn.: MBI, 2003.

Morse, Jenifer Corr. *Military Vehicles.* Speed! Woodbridge, Conn.: Blackbirch Press, 2001.

Internet Sites

FactHound offers a safe, fun way to find Internet sites related to this book. All of the sites on FactHound have been researched by our staff.

Here's how:

1. Visit *www.facthound.com*
2. Type in this special code **0736837779** for age-appropriate sites. Or enter a search word related to this book for a more general search.
3. Click on the **Fetch It** button.

FactHound will fetch the best sites for you!

Index